Waiting in Joyful Hope

Daily Reflections for
Advent and Christmas

2(

Daniel G.

LITURGICAL PRESS
Collegeville, Minnesota

www.litpress.org

Nihil Obstat: Reverend Robert Harren, J.C.L., *Censor deputatus.*
Imprimatur: ✠ Most Reverend Donald J. Kettler, J.C.L., Bishop of Saint Cloud, February 26, 2019.

Cover design by Monica Bokinskie. Cover art courtesy of Getty Images.

Daily Scripture excerpts in this work are from the *Lectionary for Mass for Use in the Dioceses of the United States of America, second typical edition* © 2001, 1998, 1997, 1986, 1970 Confraternity of Christian Doctrine, Inc., Washington, DC. Used with permission. All rights reserved. No portion of this text may be reproduced by any means without permission in writing from the copyright owner.

Other Scripture texts in this work are taken from the *New American Bible, revised edition* © 2010, 1991, 1986, 1970 Confraternity of Christian Doctrine, Washington, D.C. and are used by permission of the copyright owner. All Rights Reserved. No part of the New American Bible may be reproduced in any form without permission in writing from the copyright owner.

Excerpts from documents of the Second Vatican Council are from *Vatican Council II: Constitutions, Decrees, Declarations; The Basic Sixteen Documents*, edited by Austin Flannery, OP, © 1996. Used with permission of Liturgical Press, Collegeville, Minnesota.

© 2019 by Daniel G. Groody
Published by Liturgical Press, Collegeville, Minnesota. All rights reserved. No part of this book may be used or reproduced in any manner whatsoever, except brief quotations in reviews, without written permission of Liturgical Press, Saint John's Abbey, PO Box 7500, Collegeville, MN 56321-7500. Printed in the United States of America.

ISSN: 1550-803X
ISBN: 978-0-8146-6364-6 978-0-8146-6388-2 (ebook)

Introduction

Shortly after I graduated from college, I wanted to explore the rich and varied geographical terrain of the United States. So I asked my friend Ed Langlois if he would be interested in riding a bicycle across the country. Though neither of us had any experience for such a trip, he agreed, and we embarked on an extraordinary adventure.

We started in Portland, Maine, and rode our bikes to the other side of the country to Portland, Oregon. We started by dipping our tires in the waters of the Atlantic Ocean and then spent the next seventy-five days riding our bikes across mountains, plains, and deserts to the waters of the Pacific Ocean. Though we learned much along the way, little did I realize that this outer journey on a bicycle would parallel an inner journey of the soul.

In many ways our life is a journey between two ports and two waters. We enter the port of this world through our birth and we depart it through our death. The waters of baptism initiate us into the journey of faith, and the rite of Christian burial—which recalls the waters of baptism—marks its completion. In between these two ports and these two waters, we live out the adventure of life. It is ours to discover as a spiritual journey that takes us along the road of the paschal mystery.

Though there were many memorable moments along the way from Portland to Portland, our trek through the desert of Idaho speaks in a particular way to our journey through Advent. Because of the intensity of the desert heat, we had to bike at times in darkness. On one occasion I remember it was so dark that we could not see the road ahead of us or beneath us. We could no longer have faith in our senses so we had to learn a sense of faith that went beyond them. With only a sliver of the moon's light to guide us, we had to learn how to develop a "night vision" that enabled us to trust a deeper light even amid the darkness that enveloped us.

Advent is a time to cultivate night vision. It involves keeping the light of hope alive even when we journey through the darkness of the world, our politics, our Church, and even our very lives. It is also a time shift to a lower gear. Though our consuming culture constantly urges us into pedaling faster—which can keep us from tuning our hearts so that we can really listen—Advent calls us to slow down in order to make room for the One who is the Way, the Truth, and the Life. It calls us to seek directions from the angels, the Spirit, and people like John the Baptist, Isaiah, and Mary, who call us to make the appropriate course corrections through conversion that leads us in the right direction. As we do so, Advent becomes a time to tune into the signals from above, to calibrate our God Positioning System (GPS), if you will, until this road of faith, hope, and love leads us to our true home in the heart of the One who is the Alpha and Omega of our journey.

Thanksgiving, 2018

FIRST WEEK OF ADVENT

Climbing the Mountain of Advent

Readings: Isa 2:1-5; Rom 13:11-14; Matt 24:37-44

Scripture:
"Come, let us climb the LORD's mountain." (Isa 2:3)

Reflection: The first time I climbed up Half Dome in Yosemite Valley, I was filled with a sense of adventure and anticipation. The first 8 miles of the hike were breathtaking, but the last 400 feet scared me to death. The slope is steep, and getting to the top meant pulling myself up cables along a bare granite face with parts that have a 50-degree pitch. With no protection on either side, the slightest slip would send me tumbling thousands of feet below.

During my initial attempt, I climbed only 100 feet before my fears overcame me, and I had to turn back. The mind and heart that brought me to this point were not enough to take me to the top. After multiple attempts, I had to slow down, reframe and repattern my mind-set in order to learn a different way. Only after I changed my approach to the journey was I able to climb higher and make it to the awe-awaiting summit.

Isaiah and the psalmist speak today of the spiritual journey as an ascent up the Lord's mountain. Advent calls us to step away from the busyness of the world, to repattern the way we think about our lives in order to attain new heights in our walk with the Lord. God's path is not centered on buying and busyness but on the business of the reign of God. This kingdom is not about war, violence, or hatred but a way of faith, love, hope, trust, and peacemaking.

Meditation: Vatican II reminded us that the Eucharist is "the summit" of the Christian life and "the source from which all its power flows." As such, the Eucharist is the most important work of the church and is at the heart of our spiritual ascent with God. It is a place from which to gain a panoramic vision of life and gain new perspective on where I have been and where I am going. In this Advent season, how can I step away from the busyness of life in order to rediscover the business of my relationship with God, especially in the Eucharist?

Prayer: Lord, help me keep my thoughts on the things that are above. Even as I spend time and energy buying gifts for others during this season, help me to invest above all in the gifts of your kingdom and the treasures of your love, your grace, and your mercy.

The Heart of Worthiness

Readings: Isa 4:2-6; Matt 8:5-11

Scripture:
"Lord, I am not worthy to have you enter under my roof." (Matt 8:8)

Reflection: In the time of Jesus, slavery was a widely accepted practice. Some slaves toiled in the fields and mines, while others were domestic servants. In the Roman Empire they were often considered more as property than as persons. With no legal rights of their own, their lives were not only difficult and short, but to their owners they were often considered as disposable.

Today's readings not only introduce us to the condition of a slave but to the heart of his master. While Jesus no doubt was moved by the sickness of the soldier's servant, he must also have been moved by the humility and concern of this centurion. He was a man of rank and social importance in the Roman army, but he was not puffed up with his own self-importance. Nor did he mistreat those beneath him. The soldier not only goes out of his way to help those who work for him, but he is remarkably aware of his own unworthiness. He does not even consider himself worthy to have Jesus come to his house and enter under his own roof.

Jesus is not put off by the unworthiness of a Gentile soldier—nor our own. Rather he looks beyond our unworthiness and sees into the heart. Like the centurion soldier, Jesus not only wants to heal people of a physical illness; he wants to heal us of the blindness that keeps us from seeing our own value—and the value and dignity of each and every person.

Meditation: Though the practice of legal slavery has largely been abolished, a significant number of people today still live in physical, psychological, and emotional bondage. Many who do demeaning work often feel so degraded and socially excluded that they can feel at times as if they are nobody to anybody. God wants to free us all from the sense of unworthiness that paralyzes us—and wants us to do the same for others. How can I let God love me today, especially where I feel unworthy? And how can I value the neglected among us through a kind word, a listening ear, or a healing gesture?

Prayer: Come Holy Spirit. Enter my heart and make it your dwelling place. Move me beyond feelings of unworthiness to a place of trust in your love and mercy. Help me to reach out to those who are ignored and neglected today, and restore in us our dignity as children of God.

December 3: Saint Francis Xavier, Priest

The Human Economy and the Divine Economy

Readings: Isa 11:1-10; Luke 10:21-24

Scripture:
The Spirit of the Lord shall rest upon him. (Isa 11:2)

Reflection: Every weekday morning at 9:30, the opening bell rings at the stock market on Wall Street and the day's trading begins. At 4:00, the bell rings again and the trading stops. In between, people buy and sell, rush and hurry in order to make capital gains on their investments.

This ritual has become a cornerstone of the marketplace, and many measure their worth by the state of the human economy. Today's readings shift our focus from the human economy to what is often referred to as "the divine economy." Whereas the human economy deals with our relationship with money, the divine economy deals with our relationship with God, particularly God's plan of salvation through Jesus Christ. While the human economy focuses on *our* efforts, the divine economy puts the spotlight on *God's* initiative and grace, which will become embodied in the promised Messiah. Isaiah reminds us that God has endowed his servant with his Spirit, and that Spirit holds a priceless treasure. This Messiah wants to freely share his riches with all who would receive him.

He reminds us that to reap the dividends of the divine economy, we too must become endowed with his Spirit, which is not the spirit of the world but the Spirit of wisdom, understanding, counsel, strength, and fear of the Lord. This means investing our time, our energy, and our hearts in the life of God. What keeps us today from seeking the riches of the gospel and the treasures of the kingdom?

Meditation: The problem with the human economy is that it leaves no time for God. It keeps us so busy rushing, doing, buying, producing, accomplishing, and achieving that little space remains within our hearts for the Messiah. When we do not invest in the divine economy by developing our spiritual lives, our inner assets dry up and our hearts become bankrupt. Moreover, God measures the health of the human economy not in terms of the rise and fall of the stock market but in the "stock" people put in caring for the poorest and most vulnerable among us.

Prayer: Lord, even as I seek to earn a living, let me not forget how to live my life. Instead of worshiping the gods of the marketplace, help me to invest my energy in what ultimately matters, especially in you and the eternal riches that flow from your love and mercy.

December 4:
Saint John Damascene, Priest and Doctor of the Church

A Picture of God's Love in Action

Readings: Isa 25:6-10a; Matt 15:29-37

Scripture:
"My heart is moved with pity for the crowd." (Matt 15:32)

Reflection: I first learned the art of photography from my father. One of the things he taught me was the art of focusing. Depending on the photos we desired, we would swap out interchangeable lenses and adjust their circular dials until the subject came into clear view. As we changed between wide-angle and telephoto sizes, we explored how to frame the big picture or get up close and personal.

In different ways, the pain and suffering in our lives often can throw our vision out of focus. We wonder how a loving God can permit the calamity of natural disasters, the injustice of poverty, or even personal trials and misfortunes. Along with our sinful condition, such evils can blur our perspective and obscure our perception of God's love at work in the world.

Today's reading, however, zooms in on the ministry of Jesus. He literally gives us a picture of God's love in action. We get a close view of who God is by seeing what Jesus does. As God's love comes into focus in the person of Jesus, we see him fulfilling Isaiah's prophecy of the coming Messiah.

He makes the lame walk, the blind see, and the mute speak. Remarkably, he does not just sit on high, detached from his people, but he feels people's pain in a very intimate way. Responding not only to their hunger but also their human needs, he heals and nourishes his people, freeing them from bondage, bringing them to wholeness, and restoring them to community.

Meditation: Jesus felt people's pain. And he feels our own. Not just from a distance but up close, in the center of his heart. Matthew uses a very specific Greek word (splanchnizomai) to speak about how Jesus was moved by his innermost depths when he encountered other people's pain. He did not retreat from their suffering but immersed himself in it, offering them empathy and compassion. Instead of anesthetizing himself, he risked, touched, and healed. Where do I need God's healing touch? Who in my world is hurting? How can I be an instrument of God's healing to people who are suffering today?

Prayer: Lord, you feel the world's pain, and you feel my own. Help me not to close myself off from those who are hurting. Grant me the courage to enter more deeply into the mystery of the cross, to persevere and to reach out to others in need.

Shaky Times and Solid Foundations

Readings: Isa 26:1-6; Matt 7:21, 24-27

Scripture:
"Everyone who listens to these words of mine and acts on them will be like a wise man who built his house on rock." (Matt 7:24)

Reflection: During my undergraduate years I took a course in geology. After studying about the earth during the semester, the professor's final words were, "If you take away nothing else from this class, remember never build a house on a hillside, near a fault zone, or on unstable soil." We learned again and again what happens when people build their residences on shaky ground. These words always echoed in the back of my mind when I moved to California. Stunning were the views from some of the cliffside homes along the coast. But cataclysmic were the events when an earthquake came or a mudslide destroyed their unsteady footings and sent them crashing to ruinous depths below.

As a carpenter, Jesus inevitably knew that stable houses need solid foundations. Beyond physical foundations, Jesus in today's readings wanted his hearers to reflect on the foundational values on which we build our lives. There are events in life that inevitably shake us up, such as an unexpected death, a sudden illness, a lapse of health, a heartbreak, or a personal crisis. Without solid footings, we easily lose faith, and everything collapses. When we build our lives only on the transitory things of the earth, our lives fall apart when crises of life hit. If we build our lives on faith, hope, and love and anchor our lives on the bedrock of the gospel, we can endure life's storms until the weather clears.

How do I respond when crisis hits?

Meditation: The word for crisis in Chinese is Wei Ji (危机). It is a combination of two characters, Wei (危, danger) and Ji (机, opportunity). The intertwining of these two concepts suggests that we must make a choice when life does not go as planned and our world falls apart. Today's readings remind us that a crisis can be a dangerous moment when we abandon our faith entirely or a new opportunity to grow deeper in it. Depending on how we respond, a crisis can either result in a catastrophic devastation or a deeper relationship with God that transforms into something new.

Prayer: Lord, when crisis hits, I often want to retreat and run away. Help me remember that you are stronger than the forces that work against me, and you will never leave me alone. May I build my life on your cross, and through your power turn even my adversities into new life.

The Divine Ophthalmologist

Readings: Isa 29:17-24; Matt 9:27-31

Scripture:
Jesus said to them, "Do you believe that I can do this?"
"Yes, Lord," they said to him. (Matt 9:28)

Reflection: As we draw nearer to the events of Bethlehem, the Advent drumbeat grows louder in the background. Today we hear more about the Messiah, who will descend from the line of David. And when he comes, he will give sight to the blind.

Today two blind men come to Jesus, and although they lack physical sight, they can see that Jesus is the Messiah, who has the power to heal them. Unlike other miracle stories in the gospels, this one comes with a twist. Jesus does not just touch their eyes and cure their blindness. Instead he asks them a direct question: "Do you believe that I can do this?"

His question suggests we can reject Jesus' offer of healing. Or even more subtly doubt his power and say, "I don't know." These blind men—like us—must be more than just passive recipients of a healing grace; they must also actively choose to accept it on their end.

We can be surrounded by God's healing power, but our ego often blinds us from seeing and accepting God's power to heal us. He knocks on the door of our hearts, but he will not enter our hearts by force. Without the decision to trust God and let him enter inside, he cannot give sight to the two blind men. Without letting him inside our own lives, he cannot give us the in-sight that he alone can deliver us from darkness.

Meditation: As Jesus asked the blind men in today's readings, he also asks us, "Do you believe I can heal you and make you well?" More often than not, our response is less likely "no" and more likely "yes . . . but." Our halfheartedness often keeps us from realizing God's healing power. Jesus too meets us in the places where we most need his mercy. Like the blind men in today's readings, we too must make a choice, not just once but every day, and confess Jesus as Lord. Do we really believe he can act in our lives and make us well?

Prayer: Lord, touch the eyes of my heart and help me believe that you can do all things. You alone have the power to heal my blindness. Touch me with your mercy so that I can see clearly, and let me be full-hearted in trusting your saving power.

December 7:
Saint Ambrose, Bishop and Doctor of the Church

The Fragrance of Tenderness

Readings: Isa 30:19-21, 23-26; Matt 9:35–10:1, 5a, 6-8

Scripture:
. . . they were troubled and abandoned, like sheep without a shepherd. (Matt 9:36)

Reflection: Last year the world spent almost $40 billion on fragrances. As a human community, we invest much in looking (and smelling) good on the outside, but the readings today bring out the importance of developing a far more important aroma on the inside. The gospel gives us a glimpse of the heart of Jesus, who feels people's pain and sense of abandonment. He is particularly moved by their lack of direction. With no one to guide them when they are lost, they are like sheep without a shepherd.

Since the beginning of his pontificate, Pope Francis has reminded us that good spiritual guides are like shepherds who smell like their sheep. They smell like them because they are close to them, and they know what genuine leadership is about: they lead from behind the flock to strengthen them; they lead from within to encourage them; they lead from in front to guide them. They reek not of power, ambition, and self-interest, but they have rather the fragrance of servants. Because they are close to the One who came not to be served but to serve, they can give their lives for others. In ways big and small, they cultivate an inner aroma of humility, gentleness, generosity, love, kindness, and mercy. Because they know how to be close to the Lord, close to his heart, they can reach out to others and be close to the people the Lord has entrusted to their care.

Meditation: What the world needs now, Pope Francis says, is a revolution of tenderness. When we let tenderness in, it softens our hearts, and it heals our wounds. Life's trials can harden our hearts, but closeness to God and closeness to others can lead us closer to our hearts' desire. Advent is a time to grow closer to God's tenderness and to prepare the way so he can enter the inn of our hearts. Where do I need God's tender touch today? How can I express tenderness to my children, my spouse, or those I meet today?

Prayer: Loving God, you are the Good Shepherd who cares for your flock. Draw me to yourself through the sweet smell of your love so that I may know the gift of your tenderness. May your grace lead me to a deeper journey to my true self and a closer connection with others.

SECOND WEEK OF ADVENT

The Road to True Freedom

Readings: Isa 11:1-10; Rom 15:4-9; Matt 3:1-12

Scripture:
"Repent, for the kingdom of heaven is at hand!" (Matt 3:2)

Reflection: One of my favorite movies is *Groundhog Day*. Beyond the humor of Bill Murray, it is a profound story about a man's search for authentic freedom. In the film, Murray plays the part of a TV weatherman named Phil Connors, who is assigned to cover the story of Groundhog Day in Punxsutawney, Pennsylvania. Caught up in his own ego inflation, he thinks the assignment is far beneath his professional dignity.

After doing the story, a snowstorm strands him in Punxsutawney, which forces him to stay in the town another day. But when his alarm goes off the next morning, he discovers it is the same day over and over again. By some accounts, he relives the same Groundhog Day for eight years, eight months, and sixteen days. Eventually he realizes that each day entails making choices that only he can make. He discovers that these choices have real consequences and ultimately determine what kind of person he becomes. After a long detour through need satisfaction, he learns something new each day, and each day he becomes a little wiser. Eventually he finds that life's meaning is found, paradoxically, not in self-fulfillment but through self-giving love.

In many different ways *Groundhog Day* is a story about repentance. As he learns the daily practice of changing his mind and converting his ways, he finds the path to his heart's desire. And as he begins making choices that align him with the bigger picture of his life, he finally wakes up. Then a new day begins.

Meditation: In today's gospel reading, John the Baptist calls people to repent. "Repentance" is a dense, heavy, theological word that for many people says everything and nothing at the same time. On the surface, repentance can seem like a call to reject ourselves. But more accurately it is about rejecting our false selves in order to become our most authentic selves: the person God created us to be. Only by changing can we find a bigger and a better way. Only by letting go of our own kingdoms can we get in touch with the bigger picture of God's kingdom.

Prayer: Loving God, help me to choose life. Guide me to let go of old mind-sets, false certitudes, and unhealthy habits that keep me in bondage. Lead me to repent of all that keeps me from you. Change in me all that is not of you so that I may become all you have created me to be.

December 9:
The Immaculate Conception of the Blessed Virgin Mary

Learning to Trust

Readings: Gen 3:9-15, 20; Eph 1:3-6, 11-12; Luke 1:26-38

Scripture: "Do not be afraid, Mary." (Luke 1:30)

Reflection: When we think of Mary, we often forget her human struggles. We don't realize that she did not have a script ahead of time or a blueprint of how events would unfold. She is given an awesome promise, but she will only find her way into it through the road of faith. As we look closer at her story in her times, how could she not be afraid? She is only about thirteen years old, too young to be taken seriously. And now, not only does an angelic being take her seriously, but God himself does! She discovers that she will conceive a son even though she has not had sexual relations. How can this be? What will Joseph say? The neighbors? Or the rabbi? *If they find out it's not Joseph's baby*, she must have thought, *what will happen?* How could "this great favor" not strike terror along with the joy in her heart? Many must have been the fears in the heart of the Virgin. But against that inner darkness, we can also see the light of her own faith shining through her response. While she had fears, she did not let them control her. Nor does she cling to shallow certainties that her life can no longer hold. Instead, she goes beyond anxiety to places of greater trust. Not once, but many times over. She will learn gradually that God is in control of her life, and he alone will bring his work to completion.

Meditation: In many ways, anxiety rules our lives today. We fret about so many things and worry about some potential harm or uncertainty on the road ahead. Mary also knew fear and the vulnerabilities of being human. Yet even when her lack of control or understanding brought fear, she did not spiral into despair. Instead she stepped out in faith, trusting that God is faithful to his promises; he alone can give the peace that is beyond all understanding. What most troubles me today? Rather than a threat, how can my anxieties be an opportunity to grow in a greater trust with God?

Prayer: Lord, lead me beyond my fears to a greater faith in you. Help me stand with Mary and surrender unreservedly to your love and care, especially amid the anxieties in my life. Like her, may Christ be born in me, and may you bring his life in me to completion.

The Church of the Lost and Found

Readings: Isa 40:1-11; Matt 18:12-14

Scripture:
"What is your opinion?" (Matt 18:12)

Reflection: In today's gospel, Jesus asks for a human opinion! Imagine: the Son of God wants our take on a story about a shepherd who leaves his whole flock for the one that loses its way.

In my opinion, it's actually a crazy idea. To leave ninety-nine sheep and expose them to the vulnerability of wild animals and other dangers is outrageous. In a financial portfolio, who would risk 99 percent of their investment for the sake of the 1 percent of stocks that were losers? Why not just cut the losses and move on?

But Jesus is not concerned about the business of profit making; he is concerned rather about the business of the kingdom. And in the economy of this kingdom, everyone matters, everyone has dignity, and everyone counts. Especially sinners.

When he asks for an opinion, he is not looking for insight for himself, as if the Son of God needed human counsel. Instead, Jesus is calling his hearers to look inside, to gain in-sight into ourselves and the state of our souls. He wants us first to measure the size of our hearts by calculating the mercy within us.

For human beings, mercy has limits. When people fail us, we write them off, reject them and abandon them. In contrast, God is uncalculating in his merciful love for each one of us. When we lose our way, he searches us out. When we turn back, he embraces us.

When he finds us, he brings us back home. In what ways have I strayed?

Meditation: Whenever I suddenly realize I lost my wallet or cell phone, my heart drops. It triggers a host of anxieties, forcing me to retrace my steps frantically until I find again what I have lost. In a related way, today's readings speak about the way God's heart drops whenever we lose our way. This text is one of many "Lost and Found" passages in the Scriptures, which remind us that in the heart of the church we are called to experience mercy and communicate it. The next time we are tempted to judge others for their moral failures, it helps to remind ourselves, "When in my sin have I been lost? When through his mercy has he found me again?"

Prayer: Lord, help me to be humble. Let me not content myself on my own inner righteousness, but help me remember that you alone are holy. Help me be slow to judge and quick to love. Change the judgmental heart within me, and transform it into a vessel that transmits your tender mercies.

The Crosswinds of Discipleship

Readings: Isa 40:25-31; Matt 11:28-30

Scripture:
"Come to me, all you who labor and are burdened, and I will give you rest." (Matt 11:28)

Reflection: When my friend Ed and I rode our bicycles from Portland, Maine, to Portland, Oregon, we started our journey by dipping our tires in the Atlantic Ocean. Then we pedaled for 3,500 miles until we reached the Pacific Ocean. Although the weather and terrain gave us many challenges along the way, no part of the trip was more challenging than South Dakota. From a distance, I thought the Great Plains would be flat roads and easy riding. But little did I realize the winds would work against us in agonizing ways. At times we biked for an hour and a half and advanced only 6 miles! Amid the futility of our efforts and the forces working against us, I remember saying to myself, "Why in the world am I doing this?" The fatigue and exhaustion made me want to dump my bike by the side of the road and give up on the journey. But the decisions we made amid our weaknesses and powerlessness were arguably the most important of our journey. When we chose to persevere—even when everything inside wanted to give up—something in our attitudes changed. When we learned to say "yes"—even though everything within us wanted to say "no"—something in our inner spirit shifted. And to our surprise, as we made these adjustments on the inside, the wind shifted in our favor on the outside. And when it did, it carried us beyond the desolation of the plains to the beauty of the Rocky Mountains.

Meditation: On the road of faith, God alone knows the winds of adversity that blow against us. Scandals in the church and society, fatigue at work, and the demands of family can all take their toll and make us want to give up. Today Jesus calls us to rest in him amid the demands of the world and the needs of others. When we continually offer up to him all that we are, even our powerlessness, we find even the winds of adversity can shift in our favor and give a peace beyond understanding and a rest the world cannot give.

Prayer: Lord, you alone rule over creation. When the winds of life wear me out, help me know you are there to strengthen me. In my powerlessness, help me turn to you. Send forth your Spirit to help me persevere and to trust in the beauty beyond the pain.

A Light that Burns in the Darkness

Readings: Zech 2:14-17 or Rev 11:19a; 12:1-6a, 10ab; Luke 1:26-38 or Luke 1:39-47

Scripture:
A great sign appeared in the sky, a woman clothed with the sun, with the moon under her feet, and on her head a crown of twelve stars. (Rev 12:1)

Reflection: By December 9, 1531, the indigenous civilization in central Mexico was in ruins. The Spanish had conquered the Aztec empire a decade earlier, and in addition to the casualties of war, smallpox had completely decimated the population. By some estimates, as many as 95 percent of the people would die within a hundred years of when the Spanish arrived. The people were so disheartened that one poet wrote, "You have killed our warriors, you have burned our cities, you have destroyed our temples, you have raped our women, and now you tell us our gods are not true. If that be true, why should we live? Let us die."

In the context of this devastation, on a mountain outside of Mexico City, the Virgin Mary appeared to a poor yet dignified native Mexican named Juan Diego. Dressed as an indigenous woman and in colors that spoke to the heart of his native spiritual heritage, she made him an unlikely messenger of new creation. She commissioned him to tell the bishop of her desire to build a temple through which she would reveal God's compassion and mercy. When he doubts his capacity and asks her to send someone of greater reputation to do the job, she entrusts him with a bouquet of flowers, enfolded in his *tilma* (overcoat) and to give to the bishop. When he lowers it in the bishop's presence, the flowers fall to the ground and the image of Our Lady of Guadalupe miraculously appears on his *tilma*. From this civilization's darkest night, God opened up a ray of gospel hope.

Meditation: "Listen and hear well in your heart, my most abandoned son," our Lady of Guadalupe said to Juan Diego in 1531. "That which scares you and troubles you is nothing. Do not let your countenance and heart be troubled. Do not fear that sickness or any other sickness or anxiety. Am I not here, your Mother? Are you not under my shadow and my protection? Am I not your source of life? Are you not in the hollow of my mantle where I cross my arms? Who else do you need? Let nothing trouble you or cause you sorrow."

Prayer: Lord, like Juan Diego, I often don't feel worthy to carry out your mission. Help me to remember that you do not need title or status to accomplish your work. Amid the world's darkness, inspire me to trust that your grace is enough and in weakness your power reaches perfection.

December 13: Saint Lucy, Virgin and Martyr

The River of Mercy and the Current of Grace

Readings: Isa 48:17-19; Matt 11:16-19

Scripture:
He is like a tree
  planted near running water. (Ps 1:3)

Reflection: I used to live in the desert of Southern California in the Coachella Valley. Amid the dry and barren territory, I was always amazed by the occasional fertile strips of green life that emanated from the few streams that flowed through the area. The typology of the scriptural territory is very similar, and it is not surprising that many biblical writers speak about their relationship with God using images like "running streams." Those who have had a daily experience of hunger and thirst find much to ponder about the connection between the living God and living waters.

The river offers us a very rich metaphor for thinking about the spiritual life. The closer we are to the river, the more God's Spirit produces life through us. The farther away we get, the more barren life becomes. The river is also an image that reminds us that there is a "flow" when we allow ourselves to live in God's love and mercy. When we are "on river," we can surrender trustingly to the current of the Spirit and don't have to cling to our ways and our agendas. Nonetheless, when we stray from God and drift from the current, we get "off river." When we distance ourselves from prayer, we lose our center, and our peace evaporates, as Isaiah notes. The more we wander from it, the more our faith, hope, and love dry up. And with it the life of the soul.

Meditation: In today's readings, we can feel Jesus' exasperation at the way people have gone "off river." They are constant complainers who found fault with everything without changing anything. John fasted, and they thought he was crazy. Jesus ate and drank with them, and they thought he was indulgent. Like many people today, they spent more time criticizing others on the outside than changing themselves on the inside. Because their hearts were closed, they could not understand John nor Jesus, even when they were right in front of them. In what ways does my own complaining keep me from listening?

Prayer: Lord, at times the demands of life pull me away from the living waters of your love, and my heart becomes a barren desert. Help me to stay on the river of your mercy, and grant me the flow that enables my inner life to bear fruit in the outer world.

December 14:
Saint John of the Cross, Priest and Doctor of the Church

The Three Comings of Christ

Readings: Sir 48:1-4, 9-11; Matt 17:9a, 10-13

Scripture:
"I tell you that Elijah has already come, and they did not recognize him." (Matt 17:11)

Reflection: Advent, traditionally, is a time to recall the two comings of Christ. Bernard of Clairvaux, however, reminds us that there are in fact three comings of the Lord. The first is his coming in the nativity; the third is his coming in glory; the second is his coming in the present moment. The first is a humble coming, when he is born in Bethlehem and dwells among us. The third is a triumphant coming, when he will judge the living and the dead. The second is a hidden coming, when he knocks on the doors of the inn of our hearts and seeks to find whether we will let him inside. "The intermediate coming is a kind of path by which we travel from the first to the final," Bernard says. "In the first Christ was our redemption; in the final he shall appear as our life. In this one, that we may sleep between the middle allotments, he is our rest and consolation."

This Advent season is a time to prepare the way for Jesus' coming into our world. The busyness of our lives, however, can often crowd him out and keep him from entering. So too can our sense of unworthiness. Yet God does not need us to be worthy before he will come inside. He does not love us because we are good; but because he is good, he loves us and wants to heal us and dwell within us. How can I make room for Christ in the inn of my heart?

Meditation: In Japan there is an ancient art form called Kintsugi. It involves repairing broken pottery with gold or other precious metals. It speaks to the need to embrace the flawed dimensions of an object and allow those imperfections to be part of its beauty, rather than something to hide. God too knows our brokenness, yet often it is something we want to keep from him. Many times it is our unworthiness that keeps us from coming closer to God or letting him come inside. What are some of the broken places in my life where I need God's golden touch?

Prayer: Lord, come into my heart. Help me to let go of the perfectionism that makes me feel I need to fix myself before I am worthy of you. Give me the courage to let you inside, the strength to know you do not reject me in my brokenness, and the faith to know your healing power.

THIRD WEEK OF ADVENT

The Gift of a New Beginning

Readings: Isa 35:1-6a, 10; Jas 5:7-10; Matt 11:2-11

Scripture:
The LORD sets captives free. (Ps 146:7)

Reflection: "Jesus Christ," Pope Francis writes, "is the face of the Father's mercy. These words might well sum up the mystery of the Christian faith." The journey into the heart of Advent, in many respects, is a journey deeper into the heart of God. In Christ we discover not only the truth about God but also the truth about what it means to be human. As God's compassion made flesh, Jesus makes the invisible God visible to the world.

In today's readings, that love becomes visible in action. We learn who Jesus is by what Jesus does. He makes the lame walk, the blind see, the mute speak, and the deformed are made whole. This list of healings brings to fulfillment Isaiah's prophecy for the long-awaited and promised Messiah, who will come to restore creation. When he does, he will heal a broken world and make it whole again. As this Messiah comes into focus in Jesus Christ, we learn that God has not just created us and then left us on our own to fend for ourselves. As Messiah, he heals us; as redeemer, he re-creates us; as Savior, he saves us.

This work of salvation begins with mercy. It is the medicine of forgiveness that heals the wounds caused by sin. It is the key that unlocks the door to our emotional prisons of guilt; it is God's command that reformats our inner hard drive so that we might rediscover who we really are as children of God.

Meditation: Everyone struggles with forgiveness. While forgiving others who have wronged us is difficult, we often face greater challenges forgiving ourselves. When we do not forgive, we remain trapped in our past, which keeps us from being truly free to live out the lives God has in store for us. Advent is a time to seek forgiveness. And forgiving ourselves is an important step in trusting God's forgiveness. We protest that we don't deserve it and are not worthy. The truth is, we're not! But God's love is greater than our darkness. Where do I need the light of God's forgiveness?

Prayer: Lord, it is hard to trust that you love me so much that you forgive me. Send forth your angels to conquer the darkness that seeks only to blame and condemn me. Help me turn to your mercy, and give me faith and courage to trust in your promises.

The Question Holds the Lantern

Readings: Num 24:2-7, 15-17a; Matt 21:23-27

Scripture:
"I shall ask you one question." (Matt 21:24)

Reflection: In the gospels, Jesus is asked 183 questions. But he only directly answers three of them. In turn he asks 307 questions. This means that for every question he answers, he asks more than 100 questions. If "Jesus is the answer," as many would say today, why does he ask so many questions? Or more specifically, why doesn't he just answer our questions! Today's reading would suggest that, as Martin Copenhaver puts it, "Jesus is not the ultimate Answer Man, but more like the Great Questioner." And through these questions Jesus holds a lantern to our hearts.

When the chief priests and elders approach Jesus in the temple today, it is not clear that they are seeking understanding. It seems more likely that they are feeling that their authority as teachers is being called into question. Recognizing their closed hearts and minds, Jesus did not argue with them in a contentious theological wrangling. As he challenges them with his questions, it would appear that Jesus is more interested in enlightening our self-understanding on the inside than our enlightening others on the outside. He seems less interested in the repetition of our shallow certainties and more interested in expanding our understanding of our beliefs. Answers can foreclose new discoveries, but questions can open up new possibilities. Jesus' approach suggests he is more concerned about the formation of our hearts and the transformation of our character that can only come about through our openness to conversion.

Meditation: During a public lecture, theologian Bernard Lonergan, SJ, once remarked, "There are two kinds of people in the world: those who need certainty and those who seek understanding." The distinction he made between need and seek is significant. The world is filled with people who are smug in their beliefs. They are often the same ones who are uncivil, uncharitable, and unforgiving. Jesus wants our trust, not our certainties. He asks us to humbly "stand-under" the mysteries of faith rather than pretend that we under-stand it completely. Not having answers need not be a threat but a doorway to new discoveries!

Prayer: Lord, grant me the humility to know how little I know. Help me not to think that I am the sole owner of the truth, but open my mind to explore new questions. Guide me to stand under the mystery of life so that I may understand better the mystery of the gospel.

Eulogy Virtues and Résumé Virtues

Readings: Gen 49:2, 8-10; Matt 1:1-17

Scripture:
The book of the genealogy of Jesus Christ, the son of David, the son of Abraham. (Matt 1:1)

Reflection: In his book *The Road to Character*, David Brooks makes a distinction between "résumé virtues" and "eulogy virtues." He maintains that résumé virtues are those qualities we develop in order to get ahead in the outer world. Eulogy virtues, however, are qualities of the inner world of character that shape not just what we do but who we are as people and how we want to be remembered.

These distinctions, Brooks argues, are rooted in an internal tension between Adam I and Adam II. "While Adam I wants to conquer the world," Brooks says, "Adam II wants to obey a calling to serve the world. . . . While Adam I asks how things work, Adam II asks why things exist, and what ultimately we are here for . . . . While Adam I's motto is 'Success,' Adam II experiences life as a moral dance. His motto is 'charity, love, and redemption' " (xii).

Today's readings help us hear the music of this redemptive dance. The gospel offers us a genealogical "overture" of important musical notes in salvation history. While Matthew traces Jesus' genealogy back to Abraham, Luke traces it back to Adam. Both remind us of the many ways we live in a tension between Adam I and Adam II.

As Advent put us in touch with our fallen nature, it also puts us in tune with our redeemed nature as revealed in Christ. In him we learn not only the truth about God but also the truth about what it means to be human.

Meditation: As we travel further along the road of Advent, we come face-to-face with our own mortality. Amid the world's darkness and instabilities, we realize our own vulnerability and need for salvation. To help put my students in touch with our human condition before God, I invite them to walk around a nearby cemetery to consider the graves of those who have gone before us. As they contemplate the headstones and epitaphs, I ask them to reflect on their own mortality. When the last chapter of my life has been written, how do I want to be remembered?

Prayer: Lord, help me to remember my days are short and that every day counts. Amid the passing things of this world, grant me the wisdom to choose well, to choose life, and to choose you. Through your grace, transform the old Adam within me into your own image and likeness.

Learning the Language of Dreams

Readings: Jer 23:5-8; Matt 1:18-25

Scripture:

. . . the angel of the Lord appeared to him in a dream. (Matt 1:20)

Reflection: Shortly after the Syrian refugee crisis started, I went to Istanbul, Turkey, on a delegation with the U.S. Conference of Catholic Bishops. On our first morning we were invited to a Mass at a Syrian Catholic Church where many refugees worshiped. The local bishop there asked if I wanted to concelebrate, and I agreed, not realizing that the Mass would be celebrated in the Syrian Rite, not the Roman Rite. When we started, I suddenly discovered it was not just a different language but an entirely different set of gestures, movements, and rituals; in no time I was completely lost in a liturgical sea.

When the bishop saw my confusion, he pointed to the Sacramentary, thinking it would offer me something of a ritual life raft. The only problem was that it was written in the four local languages: Syriac, Arabic, Turkish, and Aramaic. I could not recognize a single word on the printed page!

I suddenly realized I had to learn how to find a way of understanding beyond the written and spoken word. As I saw a mosaic of the Sacred Heart, a cup with wine and bread of the altar, I realized I was part of a larger story. There was a deeper language at work that called me to trust beyond the spoken words. As these refugees shared their stories and their dreams after Mass, I realized a far deeper discourse was going on. They helped me see a unity beyond difference, a message beyond spoken utterances, and a communication beyond thought.

Meditation: In addition to the dreams that people like refugees have for a better life, the Bible has much to say about the way God speaks to us through dreams. Especially when faced with complex choices, the Bible makes note of several significant figures who find guidance through their dreams. "Dreams," says John Sanford, "are God's forgotten language." They put us in touch with a form of communication that is both deeply personal and universal at the same time. Have I ever had dreams that have shaped my choices? How can my dreams lead me to a deeper journey with God?

Prayer: Lord, give me a heart that helps people realize their dreams and the wisdom to understand my own. Grant me the discernment to understand the language of my soul and the ways you guide me through my dreams. Through them may I find healing, wholeness, and guidance in my life.

Learning to Let Go

Readings: Judg 13:2-7, 24-25a; Luke 1:5-25

Scripture:
"How shall I know this?" (Luke 1:18)

Reflection: When I was about eight years old, I found a pamphlet that posed a provocative question that I've never forgotten. It said, "Did you know you could actually miss heaven by eighteen inches?" As I read further, it explained that about a foot and a half separates the head from the heart and that God is not just an idea to give assent to with our minds but a Person to encounter in the depths of our innermost being.

In Luke's gospel we get a glimpse of this eighteen-inch journey of both Mary and Zechariah. They share much in common: both are troubled when the angel Gabriel appears; both are told not to be afraid; both are given the name of their child; both are promised the Holy Spirit; and both ask a question in response to the good news of the angel.

Despite their similarities, the angel looks favorably on Mary's response while Zechariah is chastised and punished. As we look closer, we see that Mary trusts the word of the angel and then asks a question, while Zechariah seems to want his question answered first and then implies that only after he will trust. Although Zechariah reminds us that God's call takes us beyond our comfort zone, Mary reminds us that faith involves first a decision to trust. Only after does understanding begin. As St. Augustine put it: "Faith is to believe what you do not see; the reward of this faith is to see what you believe."

Meditation: In my early twenties I learned how to rappel down a mountain. My guide first brought me to the edge of a cliff and instructed me to wrap myself in a nylon harness and thread a rope through a metal figure eight. Paradoxically, when I held on to the rope, I began to fall; when I let it go, the figure eight held me solidly in place. Only after letting go did I discover a power that sustained me beyond my own strength.

Where is God calling me to surrender my need for certainty and trust in his promises?

Prayer: Lord, like Zechariah I trust you, but my need for control often gets in the way. Help me to let go of my need for certainty and surrender without fear. Like Mary, grant me the grace to trust your promises, even if there is much I do not understand.

When the Angel Moves On . . .

Readings: Isa 7:10-14; Luke 1:26-38

Scripture:
Then the angel departed from her. (Luke 1:38)

Reflection: The State of Oregon has a rich and diverse topography. When biking through the region, I was struck by its varied terrain. At times I meandered on roads that passed through deep woods and green wilderness. And within a short distance I was traversing through vast deserts and dry places. These alternating spaces between mountain forests and desolate places echo an inner, spiritual topography as well. Sometimes our journey can feel rich and fertile. Other times our journey can feel dry and desolate.

The Scriptures today highlight that Mary's own journey with God went through alternating terrain as well. Mary inevitably knew times of closeness to God when an angel appeared to her. But the text also notes that at some point the angel left her. While we don't know the details, we can only wonder what kind of trials she endured. Imagine her thoughts when she, Joseph, and Jesus wandered in Egypt when fleeing Herod's armies. Her time in Nazareth must have seemed far away!

It is precisely in the most difficult times—when it seems like God's angels have left us—that our faith is most tested.

It is easy to believe in God when he feels close. But it's harder when he feels distant and remote and the path ahead seems uncertain. Mary's own experience reminds us that our life inevitably involves more than peak experiences and spiritual consolation; it will also involve times of dryness and desolation.

When I hit dry spots on my journey of faith, how do I respond?

Meditation: The Basilica of the Annunciation in Nazareth is the largest Christian church in the Middle East. Outside, it is crowned by a lantern-shaped cupola that gives expression to Jesus Christ as the Light of the World. On the inside, however, it is a relatively dark place. But underneath the cupola is a hole opening to the heavens, where light penetrates the inner darkness and shines directly above the cave where tradition believes that Mary lived. There she lived through alternating moments of consolation and desolation. Today she reminds us that even when we pass through deserts, God is still at work.

Prayer: Lord, help me to trust you are there even when the angels depart. Penetrate the darkness with the light of your Word. Amid the trials of life, grant me a faith that trusts beyond feelings, a hope that believes beyond sight, and a love that gives beyond my own agendas.

December 21:
Saint Peter Canisius, Priest and Doctor of the Church

Rejoicing in the Gift of Others

Readings: Song 2:8-14 or Zeph 3:14-18a; Luke 1:39-45

Scripture:
Mary set out in those days and traveled to the hill country in haste to a town of Judah. (Luke 1:39)

Reflection: The Scriptures only give us a few details about Mary's life. Some of the most revelatory come forward in today's readings, where the spotlight of God's saving love shines directly upon her. She has just received news from the angel that God highly favors her and that she will play a central role in the plan of salvation. But she is overwhelmed and unclear about how such a marvelous promise will be realized through her. It is a spiritual experience so penetrating that it scares her. Not only will she be called to live into the lonely space of being a virgin mother, but she will enter more deeply into that virgin space of intimacy between every creature and his or her Creator. While she acknowledges the impulse to pull back in fear, she chooses to leap forward in faith, trusting in God's faithfulness.

Even in her loneliness, however, she discovers she is not totally alone. She learns that her cousin Elizabeth is also a part of this plan, and leaving her security behind, she travels in haste to see her. Though she will have to travel for four days and almost one hundred miles, the difficulties do not dissuade her. All that matters now is collaborating with grace and walking with anyone committed to the coming of God's kingdom. What unfolds is one of the great examples of spiritual friendship in the Scriptures, of two lives centered in God, anchored in love, and united in a common journey together.

Meditation: In many ways our world today is defined by competition. We hail winners and shun losers and desperately seek to tally up our successes, victories, and trophies. When this mentality enters into our relationships and we seek to be better than everybody else, we lose sight of our fundamental interconnectedness. With Elizabeth and Mary, there is never a hint of social—or even spiritual—competitiveness. They see the bigger picture of God's kingdom and their place within it. They do not seek to be the center of attention but rather to center their attention on God's call, God's will, and God's grace.

Prayer: Lord, help me rejoice not only in the gifts you have given me but also the gifts you give to those around me. Open the eyes of my heart to see the bigger picture of your kingdom and to labor with you in the work of salvation.

FOURTH WEEK OF ADVENT

Keeping the Heart Open

Readings: Isa 7:10-14; Rom 1:1-7; Matt 1:18-24

Scripture:

Joseph her husband, since he was a righteous man, yet unwilling to expose her to shame, decided to divorce her quietly. (Matt 1:19)

Reflection: Joseph is in an impossible bind. He is publicly committed to Mary, but they were not yet formally married. Now she is pregnant out of wedlock. Joseph's angst becomes clearer as we realize the dilemma he faces. If Joseph says nothing, he admits of illicit sexual relations, which carried a severe social stigma. If he denies responsibility for the child, he risks exposing Mary to shame and even capital punishment (Deut 22:23-24), as the law stipulated. As a righteous man, he did not want to disregard God's laws. But as a compassionate man, he did not want to disgrace and humiliate Mary. Discerning God's will in light of what his heart believed and his religion required must have been agonizing. Caught between two opposing goods and seeing no way out, he makes an initial decision to exit out the back door by divorcing Mary quietly.

While we do not know the details of Joseph's inner struggle, we do know that when he goes to bed, he keeps his heart open. In his sleep God eventually shows him that he has more options than immediately appear. Like Joseph, we can find ourselves struggling with decisions where we do not always understand what is happening or how to decide when there seem to be no good options. When we live with humility and trust, however, God finds a way to get through to us, either through a friend, an event, a moment of illumination, or, as with Joseph, through a dream.

Meditation: Too often we think being righteous is about being "right." Yet people who need to be "right" have done countless wrongs throughout history. And it is no different today. Biblical righteousness is far deeper. It requires more than legal and moral certitudes but rather deals with faith and trust. Paul reminds us that true rightness comes through faith in the One who alone is righteous. Faith ultimately is a leap into the unknown, a surrender of trust in the God who has the power to forgive us, reconcile us, and restore us to right relationship with God and one another.

Prayer: Lord God, ruler of the universe, grant me wisdom. Especially when life presents me with difficult choices, enlighten me with your Spirit, and guide me to choose in accord with your heart. Like Joseph, may I trust in your providential care as your will unfolds in my life.

December 23: Monday of the Fourth Week of Advent

The Uncalculating Generosity of God

Readings: Mal 3:1-4, 23-24; Luke 1:57-66

Scripture:
"He will sit . . .
Refining them like gold or like silver
that they may offer due sacrifice to the LORD." (Mal 3:3)

Reflection: When I was at the Shrine of Guadalupe in Mexico some years ago, I came upon a woman sitting in the main plaza and selling some religious goods. Though it is common practice to bargain, I have never felt comfortable wrangling for the lowest price, especially when it comes to buying religious goods. I saw one piece of artwork that I liked, and I asked her the price. I felt uneasy with how little it cost and thought that, in justice, both the artist and the vendor deserved more. So I gave her more money than the asked-for price. The woman was confused at first and thought I had made a mistake, but I told her to keep the rest. She responded by giving me a hand-crafted rosary. For that I gave her more money, and she responded by giving me another gift. This practice continued a few times when we realized we were both trying to outdo each other in generosity. It was as if we were trying to refine our offering, as highlighted by Malachi in today's readings. Imagine what our world would be like if—instead of clinging to what we have and our self-interested motives—we gave it away? What if we measured our wealth not by what we have but by what we give away to one another? No matter how generous we try to be with people, however, God will never be outdone in generosity. God measures out to us the measure we give to others. The more hearts expand, the more God can pour his blessings into them, "a good measure, packed together, shaken down and overflowing."

Meditation: When we hear the word "economy" we often think of the ways goods are traded, money is exchanged, and compensation is given for what we have earned, achieved, and accomplished. The "economy" of God's kingdom, however, is different. Its primary "currency" is not merit but mercy. Salvation, above all, is an unmerited gift, not a prize we have earned. Today's readings recall the uncalculating generosity of God's grace, which he offers even though we are not worthy. Our call to love others is ultimately not based on another's response to us; it is rather a response to the God who has first loved us.

Prayer: Lord, grant me a greater sense of the abundance of your gifts and the way you are generous to all, both the deserving and the underserving. Help me to love others not to get something in return but to imitate your goodness to all creation.

Changing the World

Readings: Morning: 2 Sam 7:1-5, 8b-12, 14a, 16; Luke 1:67-79

Scripture:
You, my child, shall . . . / give his people knowledge of salvation / by the forgiveness of their sins. (Luke 1:77)

Reflection: When passing through Grand Central Station in New York some time ago, I noticed a woman sitting on the side of a wall and slumped over her knees. She had stringy gray hair and a blue faded jacket and looked like a lifeless shell. After grabbing two cups of coffee, I sat down next to her. "How are you doing?" "Fine," she said defensively. "How's your day been?" "Good!" she said guardedly. "What's new?" "Nothing!" With those words our conversation ended, and it felt like an iron wall came between us that would not let out even a pinhole of emotional light. But I stayed beside her sipping my coffee and did not leave. After about fifteen minutes she turned to me and said, "Who the hell are you anyways?" I took a sip from my cup and said, "I'm a priest, and I thought you needed a cup of coffee." With that, something unexpected happened. She began to cry with such intensity that her tears could have flooded the floors of the whole station. Not wanting to interfere with words, I just sat with her in silence while she wept and sobbed. But when she calmed down, she told me her name was Sara. I then said, "Sara, if you could change one thing in the world today, what would you change?" Surprisingly, she said, "If I could change one thing in the world today, I would change . . . my mind. I've been filled with such bitterness and hatred that I cannot forgive, but if I could, I would be a new person!"

Meditation: The Lord meets us first in mercy. He comes to bring wholeness, not condemnation. He desires healing, not judgement. He seeks to liberate us, not degrade us. He wants us to make room for him in our hearts so he can do the work only he can do. When our guilt and hurt locks us in a prison of shame, God comes to us, offering us forgiveness and new life. As the dawning of Christmas morning approaches, where is the darkness in my life that needs forgiveness? Who also do I need to forgive?

Prayer: Lord, you came to release prisoners from bondage, and so often I feel I am bound by hurts of the past, fears of the future, and anxieties in the present. Liberate me from all that holds me captive so that I may know the freedom of being a child of God.

SEASON OF CHRISTMAS

The Door of Humility

Readings:
VIGIL: Isa 62:1-5; Acts 13:16-17, 22-25; Matt 1:1-25 or 1:18-25
NIGHT: Isa 9:1-6; Titus 2:11-14; Luke 2:1-14
DAWN: Isa 62:11-12; Titus 3:4-7; Luke 2:15-20
DAY: Isa 52:7-10; Heb 1:1-6; John 1:1-18 or 1:1-5, 9-14

Scripture:
The Word became flesh / and made his dwelling among us. (John 1:14)

Reflection: The Church of the Nativity in Bethlehem was originally built in 339, and it was erected over the cave where tradition believes that Jesus was born. It is one of the oldest Christian shrines in the world, yet even today is remarkably unassuming in outward appearance. Given its importance, one might expect a majestic entrance, such as at St. Peter's Basilica in Rome, whose main doors are twenty-five feet tall. This space, however, is disarmingly simple. Its lone door is four feet high and two feet wide. To go inside and see the place where Christ was born, one has to first lower oneself and pass through this "Door of Humility." While historians argue it was designed to prevent horse- and camel-riding looters from pillaging the church at the time of the Crusades, its figurative renderings offer much material for spiritual reflection. The door also helps us understand the way the

God of the Universe lowered himself by entering into our broken, human condition. The proud and haughty cannot understand this mystery, nor can those puffed up by their own uprightness; only those who know their own unworthiness have the wisdom to bow down before entering into this sacred space. The magi were the first to contemplate this mystery and to bow before the King of kings. Paradoxically, they realized that only by bowing down could they be raised up; only by sharing their own treasure could they be enriched beyond measure; and only by leaving their own kingdoms behind could they enter the kingdom of God.

Meditation: Most Christians have no trouble believing that Jesus was God. They often have more trouble grasping that he was also a human being. The incarnation reminds us that Jesus Christ is both fully divine and fully human. This means he also knew the struggles that went with all that is involved with being human. The reason Jesus came was not just to teach us how to get to heaven. He also came to teach us how to become fully human as we journey through this world.

Prayer: Draw me more deeply Lord into to your gentle and humble heart. Help me to become more of myself and more authentically human. Repattern my thoughts and actions so that I may know the freedom and joy of being transformed into your image and likeness.

December 26: Saint Stephen, the First Martyr

"I Am a Christian!"

Readings: Acts 6:8-10; 7:54-59; Matt 10:17-22

Scripture:
As they were stoning Stephen, he called out "Lord Jesus, receive my spirit." (Acts 7:59)

Reflection: When I was doing some research at a refugee camp in Bulgaria a few years ago, a young man came up out of nowhere and said to me, "I am a Christian." Surprised that his first words to me were so bald and direct, I asked him, "Why are you a Christian?" He said, "They (ISIS) came up to me while I was living in Syria and asked me, 'Are you a Christian?' And I said, 'Yes!' And when they asked why, I said, 'I am a Christian because I want peace. I am tired of the war and the violence, and only Christ can give lasting peace.'" When he returned home later that day, a crowd of people were huddled in front of his house, and as he went inside, he found that ISIS had killed his mother, his father, and his entire family.

Martyrs lived not only in the early church, but they live today as well. While the Christmas season evokes candy canes and cookies, the liturgical calendar is sober in placing the feast of the first Christian martyr within twenty-four hours of its celebration of Jesus' birth. Lest we become overly sentimental, this feast reminds us that our faith demands a full-hearted and committed yes, not just a token and ceremonial remembrance. We may not undergo such dramatic violence and persecution as many do today, but it still summons us to witness to the God of peace, even and especially amid the violence that seeks to tear our world apart.

Meditation: "Peace is more than the absence of war," Vatican II notes, but "it is . . . 'the effect of righteousness' " and "the fruit of love." It requires not only the exercise of an outer authority but the development of an inner authority that comes from mastering the inner passions that tear us apart from within and take away our peace. In response to the violence thrust against him, Stephen entrusted his life to God, and in the end he prayed, "Lord Jesus, receive my spirit." Amid our own conflicts, peer pressure, and misunderstandings, how do we seek to find peace?

Prayer: Lord, when people turn against me, it is so easy to react and retaliate rather than respond with faith and love. Grant me a heart like St. Stephen that trusts in you, even when it costs me, to persevere even when it is difficult, and to seek the peace that only you can give.

The Twelfth Man and the Power of Love

Readings: 1 John 1:1-4; John 20:1a, 2-8

Scripture:
They both ran, but the other disciple ran faster than Peter and arrived at the tomb first. (John 20:4)

Reflection: I live and work in a place that has a long tradition of football. On game day, whenever the team faces a critical play, the home fans rise to their feet and shake their keys in their hands to help spur the eleven members of the team toward the end zone. This spirited ritual has become so integral to motivating the players that some now refer to the home crowd as the "twelfth man" on the team.

Today's readings give us insight into the way the first community of disciples came together—and the way they ran. We read especially the way Peter and the "other disciple" ran to the empty tomb—and how the other disciple ran faster than Peter. Of all details to recount at the dawn of this cosmic event unfolding in our midst, it seems odd that the evangelist would make mention of how one disciple ran faster than the other, as if an intra-disciple athletic contest would even matter!

Until we realize that the one who ran faster was the Beloved Disciple. Along with Mary, he reminds us in the long run it is love that really matters because it is love that is key to the whole human story.

Because he knows he is loved, he is empowered, not only to run physically but to run as Paul says, to win the prize and discover that our Redeemer lives—and his victory over the grave is the greatest victory of all!

Meditation: In North America, these days are marked by bowl games and football competitions. They involve times of training and coaching, fumbling and scoring and losing and winning. As much as these events are a time to showcase talent, discipline, and grit, the Scriptures today invite us beyond our television sets to see the bigger picture. The gospel holds out a vision of life that is not about a competition where one wins and the other loses but about running a race that is empowered by love. How can my own memory of love strengthen my steps to love and serve others?

Prayer: Lord, you loved your disciples with a love that was stronger even than death. May your love empower my steps and strengthen me to overcome all adversity. Help me discover anew the love that bears all things, believes all things, hopes all things, and endures all things (see 1 Cor 13:7).

December 28: The Holy Innocents, Martyrs

The Love of Power and the Power of Love

Readings: 1 John 1:5–2:2; Matt 2:13-18

Scripture:
"Herod is going to search for the child to destroy him." (Matt 2:14)

Reflection: When he receives word that a new king has been born in his jurisdiction, King Herod has a troubling sense that this One has the authority to unseat him. As he sweats and panics, one can only imagine Herod's inner discourse: *What will happen if I am no longer king? What will others say? Who will I be if all these privileges are taken from me?*

Fearful he will lose his throne, he clings to the power he thinks he has and takes extreme measures to preserve it, even to the point of killing all the children under two years old. His love for power has so consumed him that it has made him a prisoner to his own passions, which will cost him his own heart.

Ruled by fear, he loses sight of the love that could save him. In its place he chooses a self-serving power that glitters with glamour but will end in shame. In contrast, the newborn King inaugurates a different kingdom, marked by a self-giving power that is hidden in humility but will end in glory. While Herod sacrifices the lives of others to save his own power, the newborn King gives up his own power in order to save others.

Both confront us with two inescapable questions: What rules our hearts? And where do we look for salvation? While Herod choses the path that leads to the love of power, Jesus reveals a new way through the power of love.

Meditation: As much as we would like to think otherwise, Herod is not an isolated historical figure. Even in our own times, there are many leaders that seek to preserve their own power at any cost, even when it means uprooting millions and sending them into another country as refugees, like the Holy Family. It is easy to point fingers at those in power, but it is more difficult to look into our own hearts and see the way we have become indifferent to those today who flee violence in their homeland and live, as the United Nations defines a refugee, under a "well-founded fear of persecution."

Prayer: "Let us ask the Lord," Pope Francis prayed in Lampedusa, "to remove the part of Herod that lurks in our hearts . . . for the grace to weep over our indifference . . . over the cruelty of our world . . . and of all those who in anonymity make social and economic decisions which open the door to tragic situations [that result in the loss of life]."

December 29: The Holy Family of Jesus, Mary, and Joseph

One Step at a Time

Readings: Sir 3:2-6, 12-14; Col 3:12-21 or 3:12-17; Matt 2:13-15, 19-23

Scripture:
Out of Egypt I called my son. (Matt 2:15)

Reflection: With Herod's armies on their donkey's tail and a target on their son's back, this new family gets off to a rough start! It would be a hard beginning for any family, let alone God's anointed Holy Family! Their privileged role in salvation history did not dispense them from the challenges, uncertainties, and vulnerabilities that are part of every human journey.

Though this story may be familiar to us, the underlying trials of this family should not be lightly glossed over. Instead of settling down, they are forcibly uprooted and flee to Egypt to avoid Herod's murderous rage. We can only imagine the many times Mary and Joseph must have thought, *Good God, if this son of ours is so special, why must we go through so much hardship?* As the drama unfolds, we can only wonder why God would allow his own family—and even his own self—to undergo such tribulation?

As we enter more deeply into this mystery, we realize that God, in Jesus, not only leaves his homeland and enters our broken world as a "divine migrant," but he and his family also become refugees! Matthew only gives us ten brief verses to describe this journey, but we know that coming out of Egypt, his story will align with Israel's own story. But this time the promise on the horizon is not only for release from physical bondage but freedom from slavery to sin and death on a journey that will lead to the road of salvation.

Meditation: Today there are more than sixty-five million people in our world like Mary, Joseph, and Jesus who are forcibly displaced from their homelands because of persecution, war, or violence. We can only imagine how the Holy Family felt when good-hearted people unsuspectingly helped them in their need and extended spontaneous gestures of support and kindness. We cannot do everything to relieve the pain of those on the move, but we can do something. How can I make a stranger feel welcome today, honor their dignity, or reach out to those near me who are living away from their homeland?

Prayer: Lord, without knowing the road ahead, the Holy Family learned how to trust you one step at a time as they navigated their way through the challenges of life. Guide me in your goodness, even when I do not know the way ahead or how you are leading me.

December 30:
Sixth Day within the Octave of the Nativity of the Lord

Becoming Better in Bitter Times

Readings: 1 John 2:12-17; Luke 2:36-40

Scripture:
She gave thanks to God and spoke about the child to all who were awaiting the redemption of Jerusalem. (Luke 2:38)

Reflection: For most of us, the Advent and Christmas seasons are a busy time. We spend a lot of energy shopping and socializing, cooking and eating, wrapping and rushing. Yet even when there are moments of renewed encounter with relatives and friends, the holidays can also be a very lonely time for many people. Memories of loved ones who have passed on, unresolved relational conflicts, and other unmet emotional needs can leave us hungry for a connectedness beyond jingle bells and mistletoe. When these inner challenges become difficult to face, we can throw ourselves into even more frenetic activity, hoping that being "productive" will make us feel better.

Today's readings however show us another way. We are introduced to a prophetess named Anna, who inevitably knew hardship and loneliness. We learn that she was a widow for more than sixty years and had a deep closeness to God that gave her hope in difficult times. Luke makes special note of her prayer and fasting. Instead of focusing on her problems, she thanked God for his generous provision. Instead of running from her loneliness, she found ways of growing in devotion to God. Instead of becoming a bitter person, she found a way to become a better one. Amid the busyness of life, she never lost sight of the "business" of her life. Through her devotion, she gained an inner sight that allowed her to look beyond the problems of life to an endless hope in the One who alone restores creation.

Meditation: If the indulgence in Christmas cookies and candy canes has left us with something of a sweet tooth hangover, then we should take some time to explore the benefits of fasting. Fasting not only helps detoxify the body, but it clarifies the mind and strengthens the spirit. Anna highlights the way such practices paradoxically can deepen our hunger for God. As this year comes to a close, take a moment to read an article about the positive benefits to fasting, and experiment with ways it can put you in touch with the hunger for a deeper journey with God.

Prayer: Slow me down, Lord, and quiet my heart. Lead me beyond my needs and wants to see the deeper hungers of my life. Like Anna, help me discover the ways that fasting and prayer can simplify my needs, strengthen my hope, and draw me closer to you.

December 31:
Seventh Day within the Octave of the Nativity of the Lord

Putting Goodness Back on Its Throne

Readings: 1 John 2:18-21; John 1:1-18

Scripture:
The light shines in the darkness, / and the darkness has not overcome it. (John 1:5)

Reflection: A number of years ago, a couple from Rwanda approached me with a challenging project. They had survived the 1994 genocide, when one million people in their country were killed in a hundred days because of ethnic clashes. Many of their own family members and friends were murdered during that genocide. Amid the madness, they took refuge in the Hotel Mille Collines, popularly known as "Hotel Rwanda" by the film of that name. They asked if I would accompany them in their search for God amid the bloodshed. I willingly agreed. But I honestly had no idea of how to authentically speak about God from so dark a context.

A team of us eventually went to Rwanda to explore this topic, and I will never forget walking through the churches where so many were massacred. Today their bones are on display in the back of these churches, where the souls of the innocent still cry to heaven for redress.

Toward the end of our time in Rwanda, we asked a religious sister what lesson humanity should learn from the Rwanda genocide. Recalling a very specific spiritual experience, she said, "In Rwanda, humanity had descended to its lowest place, and I experienced fear like never before. God did not take away these fears," she said, "but he gave me the strength to go through them. And from this darkest place, I heard God calling me to be a messenger of light and hope and to put goodness back on its throne."

Meditation: As the darkness of the world today confronts us, it is easy to feel overwhelmed and powerless. Not only do we not know where to begin, but we wonder if our efforts to combat the evil around us will even make a difference. Our readings today remind us that our hope rests not in seeing tangible results from our efforts but in trusting the One who we confess as the Light of the World. As I await the dawning of a new year, in what ways can I look toward being light in the midst of world's darkness and put goodness back on its throne?

Prayer: Loving God, you enter into the darkest places of the human heart and open up a way to hope for every creature. Let your goodness reign in my heart, and help me to be a visible embodiment of the love you have for all, especially those most in need of your grace and mercy.

January 1: Solemnity of Mary, the Holy Mother of God

The Bethlehem-Manger Plan

Readings: Num 6:22-27; Gal 4:4-7; Luke 2:16-21

Scripture:
The shepherds went in haste to Bethlehem and found Mary and Joseph, and the infant lying in the manger. (Luke 2:16)

Reflection: I teach a college-level course on foundations of theology. When we begin studying the New Testament, I ask students to consider what it would be like if God just appointed them as members of his senior advisory council. At their first gathering God asks their input on how to save humanity from its own self-destruction. The only condition is they have to respect free will. Their insights are, in a word, "revelatory."

Some come up with a "shock and awe" option that would force people to cower into submission after seeing God's power. Others propose a "fame and status" option where a celebrity delivers God's message to make it more "credible." Still others propose something of a "divine bitcoin" option where people earn their way into a new kingdom through a quasi-good-works currency. Of all the possibilities, however, no one dares to suggest the "Bethlehem manger" option where God gratuitously offers his mercy to all. Who would think the way to save the world would be through a child in a manger? Or to anoint shepherds as first messengers of this good news? Most would have ruled it out as impractical, unworkable, and even dangerously naïve!

God's entrance into our world in such a lowly estate should challenge and rework all our conventional mind-sets. Our faith tells us he will return in glory. But now he invites us close to him in his humanity and vulnerability. Inseparable to this mystery is the person of Mary, whose "yes" to God unraveled the knot of sin and made possible a new creation.

Meditation: We begin this new year honoring Mary the Mother of God. What a title for a simple girl from Nazareth! She is recognized by many names throughout history, but Pope Francis has promoted in particular a devotion to Our Lady, Undoer of Knots. A novena in her name brings out that, if Eve through her disobedience tied the knot of sin that is at the root of all human problems, then Mary as the new Eve has the power to undo the complicated problems of our lives if we surrender them to her. As we begin this new year, what knots in my life need Mary's unraveling help?

Prayer: Lord, too often I try to do everything myself and am too proud to ask for help. Only you can save us. Help me to discover anew your power to bring new life, and with Mary's help, undo the inner knots that keep me from being free.

January 2: Saints Basil the Great and Gregory Nazianzen, Bishops and Doctors of the Church

Making Room for Christ

Readings: 1 John 2:22-28; John 1:19-28

Scripture:
"I baptize with water; but there is one among you whom you do not recognize, . . . whose sandal strap I am not worthy to untie." (John 1:26-27)

Reflection: Fr. Joe Pawlicki, CSC, worked among the migrants in the Coachella Valley of Southern California for decades until he passed away in 1999. He founded a retreat program called the Valley Missionary Program, and it has had a tremendous transformative effect on the lives of tens of thousands of people. One night, before a retreat began, I was stunned by the thunderous applause that welcomed him when he walked into the room. Later that night we got together, and I asked him about how he understood his ministry. "It's not about the big crowds, nor people's praise," he said to me. "When I first started this work, I was asked to give a talk at a parish about four hours from home. It took a lot of effort to prepare and travel there, and I expected a lot of people would come. But when I got there, only one person showed up. In my disappointment and frustration, I said to God, 'Why did you bring me all the way out here for just one person?' " At that moment he felt God saying to him, *This is what it's all about Joe: ministering to people one person at a time.* From that insight, he built a retreat program based on a one-on-one model of evangelization. His ministry was fruitful because he always understood his ministry within the bigger picture, which was not to put the spotlight on him but to lead people to the One who alone is the Light of the World.

Meditation: John the Baptist had such a clear sense of the big picture of God's kingdom that he saw himself as insignificant in comparison, so much so that he did not consider himself worthy even to untie the Messiah's sandals, which was a slave's work. Despite the crowds he attracted, John realized his ministry was not about him but about Jesus. In our own work, we can easily be tempted to use others to serve our own needs rather than others' needs. In what ways do I try to be the center of attention rather than to center my attention on Jesus?

Prayer: "As a Christian, I am called on to be another Christ; therefore I must empty myself of me to make room for Him. Woe be it unto me if my brothers and sisters should come looking for Christ, and instead they find only me."

January 3: Thursday before Epiphany
(The Most Holy Name of Jesus)

The Divine Stain Remover

Readings: 1 John 2:29–3:6; John 1:29-34

Scripture:
John the Baptist saw Jesus coming toward him and said, "Behold, the Lamb of God, who takes away the sin of the world." (John 1:29)

Reflection: The story of William Shakespeare's Macbeth revolves around one couple's desire for power—and the price they are willing to pay for it. The title character is a successful soldier, but his ambitious wife, Lady Macbeth, conspires to kill the present king Duncan so that her husband may ascend to the throne. Lady Macbeth underestimates the cost of this crime on her own soul, however, and as the narrative unfolds she is tormented by her guilt. In the latter part of the story she sleepwalks through the castle in a stuporous guilt, and imagining the king's blood on her hands, she tries to wash it away with the famous words, "Out damned spot! Out, I say!" No matter how hard she tries, she cannot remove the spot of her misdeeds by her own power.

When John the Baptist emerges in today's readings, he recognizes the only One that can remove the spot that stains the conscience of every human being. Even John, in all of his holiness, did not have the power to remove it. When he names Jesus as the Lamb of God, he is alluding to Israel's hope of liberation (see Exod 12) and the prophet's prediction of a suffering servant (see Isa 53). In time the book of Revelation will speak of the final promised victory of this Lamb, who removes the stains, washes the robes and makes them white through his own blood (see Rev 7:13). Where do I need the Lamb's redemptive touch to remove the stain of sin?

Meditation: Guilt is not easy to face. But it is impossible to ignore. If we don't deal with it, it deals with us. Jesus came to take away that guilt and to remove the stain on the inner garments of our soul. When we hear the words "Behold, the Lamb of God" in the liturgy, it is an opportunity to not only enter more deeply into Israel's story but our own story. Though we are not worthy to receive this mercy, God freely shares it. Spend some time with the words "How happy are we who are called to the supper of the Lamb."

Prayer: Lord, you came not to be served but to serve and to give yourself as a ransom for many. Help me to love others with the love with which you have loved me, and may I look on my own life and on others with the eyes of your mercy.

Engaging the Heart's Desires

Readings: 1 John 3:7-10; John 1:35-42

Scripture:
Jesus turned and saw them following him and said to them, "What are you looking for?" (John 1:38)

Reflection: One of the classes I teach is called "The Heart's Desire and Social Change." It is a chance for university students to explore the connection between the deepest desires of their hearts and the needs and challenges of the world. More often than not students can identify a global issue in the "outside world" that challenges them, but frequently they have more difficulty working through the issues of their "inside world." Without periodically disengaging from the busyness of daily life, it is hard to listen to what is stirring within us.

When Jesus first sees John the Baptist's disciples in today's gospel, he asks them about their heart's desires: "What are you looking for?" In turn they also ask him a question, but it is not "What are we to do?" They ask first about where he dwells, where he lives in his innermost heart.

The first disciples remind us that following Christ begins with dwelling in Christ, entering the place of his loving embrace, staying under the gaze of his tender mercy. It involves living with a heart open to love, a heart willing to change, a heart ready to serve, a heart disposed to listen. They help us remember that the world is hungry not for busier people but bigger-hearted people who are so at home with God that they become a doorway into God. Following Jesus begins with learning to dwell in love and to seek above all a closeness to the Father's heart.

Meditation: In a time when our hearts and minds are pulled in so many directions, it is easy to confuse our wants with our deepest desires. Jeremiah chastises the people of Israel because of two evils: ". . . they have forsaken me, the source of living waters; They have dug themselves cisterns, broken cisterns that cannot hold water" (Jer 2:13). In order to keep growing closer to God, we have to spend time with God. As this new year begins, how can I enter a livelier rhythm that makes time to dwell with God?

Prayer: Lord, often my needs and desires take me too many places, and I lose track of what really matters. Teach me, through my experience of what really endures, to ground myself on the desires that lead to you, and to set my heart on your kingdom.

EPIPHANY AND BAPTISM OF THE LORD

The Hidden Treasures

Readings: Isa 60:1-6; Eph 3:2-3a, 5-6; Matt 2:1-12

Scripture:

Magi from the east arrived in Jerusalem, saying, "Where is the newborn king of the Jews? We saw his star at its rising and have come to do him homage." (Matt 2:1-2)

Reflection: When God descended to earth in Jesus, a star ascended in the heavens, signaling that something powerful had happened in the cosmos. The magi see this celestial event and are astounded. In response they leave behind what they have, move out of their comfort zones, and set forth on an unknown path. What was it that inflamed their hearts and led them to leave their homelands and migrate to a foreign territory? Even when they do not know the way, they know their place in the universe and that their lives are at the service of the bigger picture of God's kingdom. They not only took great risks, but they went out in search of a treasure that was greater than their earthly riches, human ambitions, or political power. They knew there was a treasure greater than this world has to offer, and they wanted to find it. Herod too receives news of this great event, but he is not willing to pay the same price. Instead of surrendering all he has been given to a greater kingdom, he frets and worries and tries to protect the small kingdom he thinks he has. Tradition holds that the magi, like Herod, were kings. But the difference between Herod and them is that they saw themselves as stewards and not owners of all that is entrusted to them. Instead of clutching what they had like Herod did, they opened their treasures and offered this newborn King gold, frankincense, and myrrh.

Meditation: The magi have been known for many things, but here they may be considered "wise" especially because of the way they understood their lives, and all they possess, within the larger frame of God's kingdom. Like Herod, a part of us seeks to cling to what we have, but the magi call us to move beyond our needs and wants in order to be more responsive to God's presence in our midst. They remind us not to worship creation but the Creator, not the gifts of this world but the One who generously gives them to us. In what ways do I make an idol of the things of this earth?

Prayer: Loving God, like Herod I often try to control my little kingdoms rather than surrender to the power of your kingdom. Loosen my grip, Lord, and rein in my heart. As magi treasured you more than anything else in this passing world, so help me to seek you above all things and know the gift of your peace.

January 6: Monday after Epiphany
(Saint André Bessette, Religious)

God's Strength and Human Weakness

Readings: 1 John 3:22–4:6; Matt 4:12-17, 23-25

Scripture:
He was the son, as was thought, of Joseph. (Luke 3:23)

Reflection: "With the smallest brushes," St. André Bessette would say, "the artist paints the most exquisitely beautiful pictures." On the canvas of this small, infirm, uneducated, and illiterate brother, God sketched the colors of his compassionate care for all creatures, especially those in suffering and pain.

While he was first rejected when he applied because of poor health, he spent most of his years in the Congregation of Holy Cross. Upon entering he was given the job as a porter at Notre Dame College in Quebec and spent forty years opening doors for students as they came to school. In time his central mission evolved into opening people to God's embrace amid their own struggle and suffering. The experience of his own weakness paradoxically strengthened his spirit and sensitized him to the pain of others. From this heart he counseled people to pray "not to be spared trials but to ask instead for the grace to bear them well." Though credited with thousands of miraculous healings, André never claimed that this power came from himself but from God alone, through the intercession of St. Joseph.

As news spread of miraculous healings, pilgrims came to visit André by the hundreds and then by the thousands. Now, almost eight decades since his death, more than two million people visit the St. Joseph's Oratory in Montreal each year. André's deep faith, devotion, and dedication witness not only to God's desire to bring wholeness to his people but also his power at work in human weakness.

Meditation: So often we think our weaknesses are impediments to God and faults we have to overcome to become more worthy and acceptable. It is not easy to practice loving-kindness, especially toward ourselves, but paradoxically, the more we accept God's acceptance of who we are, the more we can practice that same loving-kindness toward others. André gives us a great window into the ways God can transform our weaknesses into strengths. What are some of the weaknesses and limitations that I currently suffer with, and how can I allow God to transform them through the cross into a gift for others?

Prayer: Lord, you chose Brother André to spread devotion to St. Joseph and to dedicate himself to the poor and afflicted. Grant us the grace to imitate his humility and charity, so that, with him, we may share the reward promised to all who care for their neighbors out of love for you.

Globalizing Solidarity

Readings: 1 John 4:7-10; Mark 6:34-44

Scripture:

When Jesus saw the vast crowd, his heart was moved with pity for them, for they were like sheep without a shepherd. (Mark 6:34)

Reflection: In the summer of 2013, an overcrowded boat of refugees departed from the North African coast and launched into the open sea. Fleeing violence and unrest, they hoped to make it to European shores. While en route their vessel capsized, however, and most of them drowned in the middle of the Mediterranean. Eight of them survived the shipwreck by clinging to fishing nets of a nearby boat. When these refugees saw fishermen in the distance, they pleaded desperately for help, but when the fishermen saw the refugees holding on to their lines, they cut them loose to die in the ocean depths.

When the newly elected Pope Francis heard this story, it moved him deeply and reached him, he said, "like a painful thorn in my heart." In response he wanted to make "a sign of . . . closeness" with those suffering and severed from the human community and to challenge the conscience of the world, "lest this tragedy be repeated." Eight days later he made his first pastoral visit outside of the Vatican to the small and isolated Italian island of Lampedusa, where, using a chalice hewn from a sunken refugee boat, he celebrated Mass and preached against the "globalization of indifference" to those suffering around us.

In today's gospel we read about Jesus' own heart breaking at the sight of people suffering. What is one issue that breaks my heart? Today, how can I make one small step to counter the "globalization of indifference" with a globalization of solidarity?

Meditation: In response to the hungry crowds, Jesus did not shy away from the world that called out to him in need. Though united to the Father's infinite care, he also experienced human limitations. He did not despair when confronted with how many came to him for healing. Like the disciples, we can frequently feel overwhelmed and powerless, that we are not enough, or do not have enough, to respond to the world's needs. Jesus called his disciples—and us—to open our hearts, to work together, and to share what we have. Instead of trying to do it all on my own, what organization can I partner with to address a critical area of human need?

Prayer: Lord, so often I get so caught up in my own world that I become indifferent to the suffering of others around me. Grant me a heart of flesh and a responsive spirit to feel like you felt at the sight of the hungry crowds, to counter the indifference of the world with compassionate generosity.

January 8: Wednesday after Epiphany

Turbulent Seas and Peaceful Waters

Readings: 1 John 4:11-18; Mark 6:45-52

Scripture:
"Take courage, it is I, do not be afraid!" (Mark 6:50)

Reflection: I've always been a bit queasy on boats. Leaving the security of land, and launching out into the insecurity of sea, has always made me uneasy. What if something happens to this fragile vessel that is holding me afloat? Today's readings take that anxiety to a new level. It is between three and six in the morning, and we find the disciples on a storm-tossed boat. The waves are crashing on the bow, the water is filling the hull, and they are still far from land. Who wouldn't be afraid? If their fear of drowning isn't enough, they then see Jesus walking on the sea, and it spooks them. But he sees their struggles, and he reaches out to them. He speaks a word, and everything goes quiet. He gets into the boat, and the winds die down. Who is this man? Mark wants us to see that Jesus is more than a miracle worker who walks on water and multiplies loaves. He is the One who has power over the forces of nature in Genesis, the One who feeds the Israelites in the desert in Exodus, and the One who calls us to believe in him. Amid our deepest anxieties and most tumultuous conflicts, he reveals himself as the God who created us, rescues us, and is with us. Even when forces threaten to capsize us, he wants us to bring him on board and respond with faith and trust in his power to save us.

Meditation: More often than we care to admit, fear frequently controls our lives and keeps us in bondage. When unexpected events cause an inner tempest, we find ourselves in the same boat as the disciples. Yet when they were afraid they wouldn't have enough food, he provided. When they were afraid they would drown, he calmed the seas. What is it that triggers my fears? How do I respond when I encounter rough waters and stormy seas? And where do they take me? As he spoke to his disciples, he speaks to us: "Take courage, it is I, do not be afraid!"

Prayer: Come into my boat, Lord, and keep my rudder steady amid the storms of my life. Grant me a faith that trusts amid the trials and a love that casts out all fear, until I cross the turbulent seas of this world and you bring me to safe harbor.

January 9: Thursday after Epiphany

Reformatting Our Inner Hard Drives

Readings: 1 John 4:19–5:4; Luke 4:14-22a

Scripture:
The Spirit of the Lord is upon me. (Luke 4:18)

Reflection: For various reasons, I periodically reformat my computer's hard drive. Software corruption, malware, and viruses lead me to erase the existing system and reinstall the original software. Once it recovers its "factory image," it works like an entirely new machine.

In today's gospel we read about Jesus' vision of mission, which is to help humanity recover its original image and likeness to God, which has been corrupted by sin. This mission reveals God's desire to redeem all humanity—not just Jews—from its poverty, bondage, and blindness. This angered those gathered in the synagogue, who thought they alone were the chosen ones of God. But Jesus challenges them to reformat their narrow and self-centered thinking and to be delivered from the poverty, bondage, and blindness that has kept them from the freedom of living as children of God. In its place he calls them to download new "software" revealed in the humanity of Jesus, who is the image of the invisible God and the firstborn of all creation.

As we hear this passage today, as once heard in a synagogue in Nazareth, it comforts us, but it also disrupts us. It comforts us because it promises us something new. But it disrupts us because it calls us to repattern our thinking from the ways of the world to the ways of God's kingdom. What patterns of thinking and acting keep me from living, thinking, and acting according to God's image and likeness?

Meditation: There are many ways that Wall Street, Madison Avenue, and Hollywood have "programmed" us to think about who we are, what we need, and what really matters. When we live by the creeds of these systems, we "buy" into the notion that everything has a price, even love. Moreover, our own fear and shame make us feel like we are not worthy of it. But today's readings reveal that God is love—and it is freely given to us without having to earn it or achieve it. Where do I need to let the light of God's love into the darkest places of my life?

Prayer: Heavenly Father, reformat my mind and heart, and download into my whole being the Spirit of your Son. May your grace transform my attitudes, values, and thinking so that they conform to your kingdom and allow me to rediscover what it means to live in your image and likeness.

January 10: Friday after Epiphany

The Divine Cardiologist

Readings: 1 John 5:5-13; Luke 5:12-16

Scripture:
"Lord, if you wish, you can make me clean." (Luke 5:12)

Reflection: When I was a seminarian I worked as a chaplain in a hospital, and one of my areas of responsibility was the cardiac unit. After speaking with patients over a period of time before and after their operations, I became curious about the process of open-heart surgery itself. At one point I asked if I could observe a surgery, and it was on many levels a contemplative experience. Not only was I deeply impressed by the technical skill of the surgeons who were able to heal the blockages in a person's system and bring her back to health, but on a more fundamental level I was awed by the miracle of the human heart itself.

The human heart is a physical organ charged with mystical qualities, and it is the privileged place of encounter between the divine and the human. But because of the wounds caused by sin, it is also a place where profound healing is needed. In today's readings Jesus reveals himself as the Divine Physician. He heals a leper of his physical illness, but he also heals him of his uncleanness. While on some level this uncleanness had to do with the way his leprosy rendered him ritually unclean according to Jewish law, it also names the inner uncleanness that every human being feels in their inner depths, especially in connection to fear and shame. Where do I need the Divine Physician's healing touch today in order to be restored to health and made clean again?

Meditation: In the gospels Jesus reveals that he has power over the forces of nature, over the forces of evil, and even over the forces of death. The one area where he chooses not to abuse his power is over the human heart. Respecting our own free will, he does not enter our hearts by force. The leper in today's readings was not too proud to ask for help, and he had the wisdom to know where he needed healing. What keeps me from letting God's healing touch into my heart and opening myself more fully to the healing he offers?

Prayer: You alone as the Divine Physician have the power to restore our hearts and make us one with you. Open my heart, Lord, and make me clean. Heal the wounds caused by sin, and may your life and love flow from you through me to others.

True Worship

Readings: 1 John 5:14-21; John 3:22-30

Scripture:
Be on your guard against idols. (1 John 5:21)

Reflection: Adolf Eichmann was one of the chief organizers of the Holocaust during the reign of the Third Reich. After World War II ended, he was captured and put on trial in Jerusalem on April 11, 1961. For 56 days the prosecution brought forth 110 witnesses and over 1,600 documents that testified to his war crimes and crimes against humanity. Afterward, Eichmann himself took the stand to present his side of the story. When he was sworn in, a New Testament was placed in front of him, but instead of putting his hand on the Scriptures, he laid it aside and said, "I do not swear by the Bible; I swear by Almighty God." How can a person who orchestrated such evil actually claim to believe in God? Or more precisely, who was Eichmann's god?

In the First Letter of John we are admonished, "Be on your guard against idols." He reminds us that one of the great human vulnerabilities is not atheism but idolatry: it is not if we believe in God or not, but it is about what god we believe in. John says that when we live in love, in truth, in life, in hope, we live in the God of Jesus Christ. What are the gods of our own times that want our attention, demand our obedience, but lead us astray? How do idols like consumerism, money-theism, nationalism, egotism, and other gods lead us away from our true selves and true worship?

Meditation: From earliest times the church has always maintained *Ecclesia Semper Reformandum* (the church must always be in reform of itself). Without continual self-examination about how its own life conforms to the life of Jesus Christ, the church falls into the idols of its own self-interest. This is not only true collectively but also personally. If we are to become an authentic reflection of the love of the living God, we must renounce the idols of our society that lead us astray and allow God to transform our thoughts, attitudes, and actions in order to become another Christ.

Prayer: Lord, so often I am resistant to change, and I want to make you into my own disordered image and likeness rather than to be transformed into your image and likeness. Give me an open heart that is willing to change so that I may become who you have created me to be.

Standing under the Gaze of Love

Readings: Isa 42:1-4, 6-7; Acts 10:34-38; Matt 3:13-17

Scripture:
"This is my beloved Son, with whom I am well pleased." (Matt 3:16-17)

Reflection: The place where Jesus was likely baptized is called today Qasr el Yahud. It is just above the Dead Sea, which is a barren place with no plants, fish, or visible signs of life. Located 1,412 feet below sea level, it is the earth's lowest elevation on land. But there is more here than a geographical note of the evangelist. It reveals that Jesus not only enters our world as a human being, but he literally meets the human race at the lowest point of our earthly existence. Amid this lifeless context, he stands underneath the Father's gaze and a voice from the heavens says, "This is my beloved Son, with whom I am well pleased."

From the lowest places of our lives, God also invites us as well to stand with Jesus under the Father's gaze, under his love and mercy. When we really dare to come close to this unapproachable light, however, we often do not think ourselves worthy, and our fear and shame would have us believe that we do not deserve it. The gospel brings forth a different story. Today's readings remind us that God loves us not because we are good but because God is good. Jesus came not for the righteous but for sinners like you and me. Living out our baptism involves living out the knowledge that we are loved without reservation and without condition. How else can we respond but to seek to love others as he has loved us?

Meditation: It takes our entire lives to accept the truth of our baptism, to realize we are God's beloved. To live under God's gaze means letting all of who we are be loved—not just our best sides! The good news consists in this: not that we are perfect but that, while we are still sinners, Christ died for us (see Rom 5:8). As sinners loved by God, we are called to be heralds of a new creation constantly renewing the world through the Redeemer's grace. To the God who created us by love, for love, and to love, let all creation say, Amen.

Prayer: Lord Jesus, you descended to the lowest point on earth so that we might know the heights and the depths of the Father's mercy. May we center our lives under your loving gaze, and live out our own baptism by making more visible the invisible heart of God.

References

December 1: First Sunday of Advent

Second Vatican Council, The Constitution on the Sacred Liturgy (*Sacrosanctum Concilium*) 10.

December 12: Our Lady of Guadalupe

Fr. Virgilio Elizondo, "Our Lady of Guadalupe: Mother of a New Creation," Habiger Lecture (St. Paul: University of St. Thomas, 2002), https://www.stthomas.edu/media/catholicstudies/center/habiger/misc/Elizondo-Spring2002.pdf.

December 14: Saint John of the Cross, Priest and Doctor of the Church

St. Bernard of Clairvaux, *Sermons for Advent and the Christmas Season*, trans. Irene Edmonds, Wendy Mary Beckett, and Conrad Greenia, ed. John Leinenweber, CF 51 (Collegeville, MN: Cistercian Publications, 2007), 33–34. This sermon is used in the Roman Office of Readings for Wednesday of the First Week of Advent. See also https://www.crossroadsinitiative.com/media/articles/three-comings-of-the-lord-st-bernard/.

December 15: Sunday of the Third Week of Advent

Pope Francis, *Misericordiae Vultus*: Bull of Indiction of the Extraordinary Jubilee of Mercy 1, https://w2.vatican.va/content/francesco/en/bulls/documents/papa-francesco_bolla_20150411_misericordiae-vultus.html.

December 16: Monday of the Third Week of Advent

I'm grateful to John O'Donohue who used the phrase, "The Question Holds the Lantern." For more on this topic, see O'Donohue, "The Question Holds the Lantern," *The Sun* (November 2009), https://www.thesunmagazine.org/issues/407/thequestion holds-the-lantern.

Martin Copenhaver, *Jesus Is the Question: The 307 Questions Jesus Asked and the 3 He Answered* (Nashville: Abingdon, 2014).

I am grateful to Fr. Dave Burrell, CSC, for this insight on Bernard Lonergan's lecture.

December 17: Tuesday of the Third Week of Advent

In his analysis, David Brooks draws on the work of Rabbi Joseph Soloveitchik (1903–1993) and his 1965 book, *The Lonely Man of Faith*. For more on this topic, see Brooks, *The Road to Character* (New York: Random House, 2015).

December 18: Wednesday of the Third Week of Advent

John Sanford, *Dreams: God's Forgotten Language* (San Francisco: HarperSanFrancisco, 1989).

December 19: Thursday of the Third Week of Advent

Augustine of Hippo, *Sermons* 4.1.1.

December 25: The Nativity of the Lord (Christmas)

Fr. Richard Rohr, OFM, "The Lost Tradition of Contemplation," Center for Action and Contemplation (January 9, 2018), https://cac.org/the-lost-tradition-of-contemplation-2018-01-09/.

December 26: Saint Stephen, the First Martyr

Second Vatican Council, Pastoral Constitution on the Church in the Modern World (*Gaudium et Spes*) 78.

December 28: The Holy Innocents, Martyrs

Pope Francis, Homily at Lampedusa (July 8, 2013), http://w2.vatican.va/content/francesco/en/homilies/2013/documents/papa-francesco_20130708_omelia-lampedusa.html.

January 2: Saints Basil the Great and Gregory Nazianzen, Bishops and Doctors of the Church

The origin of the quote in the prayer is unknown, but I first received it from Fr. Dave Link.

January 7: Tuesday after Epiphany

Pope Francis, Homily at Lampedusa (July 8, 2013), http://w2.vatican.va/content/francesco/en/homilies/2013/documents/papa-francesco_20130708_omelia-lampedusa.html.

SEASONAL REFLECTIONS NOW AVAILABLE IN ENGLISH AND SPANISH

LENT/CUARESMA

Not By Bread Alone: Daily Reflections for Lent 2020
Michelle Francl-Donnay

No sólo de pan: Reflexiones diarias para Cuaresma 2020
Michelle Francl-Donnay; Translated by Luis Baudry-Simón

EASTER/PASCUA

Rejoice and Be Glad: Daily Reflections for Easter 2020
Mary DeTurris Poust

Alégrense y regocíjense: Reflexiones diarias para Pascua 2020
Mary DeTurris Poust; Translated by Luis Baudry-Simón

Standard, large-print, and eBook editions available. Call 800-858-5450 or visit www.litpress.org for more information and special bulk pricing discounts.

Ediciones estándar, de letra grande y de libro electrónico disponibles. Llame al 800-858-5450 o visite www.litpress.org para obtener más información y descuentos especiales de precios al por mayor.